To Kaye, as always

Edited by Vreni Merriam and Marsha Weese

Copyright © 2013 by John Merriam

Published by University Book Store Press
Printed on the Espresso Book Machine
4326 University Way NE
Seattle, WA 98105
www.ubookstore.com

ISBN: 978-1-937358-30-3

THE LAST VOYAGE OF THE S.S. PRODUCER
(dedicated to the memory of E. Michael Costello)

by John Merriam

It's been over 40 years since I joined the S.S. Producer. I've forgotten a lot of the detail that makes for a good yarn. But I had to wait until now to tell it. I still can't tell you everything I know because some of the characters, including me, are still alive. This story is for Mike Costello. R.I.P.

The first time I met Mike was when he walked out of the desert in Bandar Abbas, Iran. The Shah was still in power when we put in to that godforsaken port. I was part of the crew for the S.S. Producer, the first U.S.-flagged merchant ship to ever visit Bandar Abbas. Mike showed up one day at the bottom of the gangway with a handtruck stacked with cases of soda, a welcome sight in that parched region of the Persian Gulf. It would be some time before I found out that disguised amongst the soda were 40 kilograms of Afghani hashish.

I

The story begins in December 1971.

I lost my student deferment from the draft during fall quarter due to low grades at the University of Washington. On December

16th I was summoned to the Selective Service Induction Center on 15th Avenue West in Seattle where I deliberately flunked the physical exam and got a 4F deferment. That's another story. Suffice it to say that, trying to stay in school, I'd been broke for a long time and needed to get a job real bad.

I had joined the U.S. merchant marine the year before and had worked on four freighters in between taking classes at the U.W. I held a B-book—second tier seniority—in the Seafarers International Union (SIU). The day after I beat the draft, I started hanging out in the SIU hiring hall at 1st and Wall in Seattle. (About 25 years later, my union hall got turned into a fancy steakhouse called El Gaucho.)

Normally shipping was good during the Viet Nam war but the longshoremen were in the middle of the longest dock strike in West Coast history. The longshoremen's union (ILWU) and the Teamsters had some sort of beef about who was going to load cargo into containers. Containerized cargo was a new concept at the time. Truckers and dock workers were trying to figure out, forcibly, who had jurisdiction—and when—over this new form of cargo. The SIU wouldn't cross picket lines thrown up by either of the unions and no ships had been moving in or out of West Coast ports since the summer.

President Nixon was upset that supplies weren't getting sent to his war in Viet Nam. He slapped a Taft-Hartley injunction on the longshoremen, forcing them back to work for an 80-day 'cooling off' period which was due to expire just after Christmas. Nixon was also trying to get Congress to pass a law making longshore strikes illegal. The times were somewhat turbulent.

That December wasn't the best time for a B-book like me to try to catch a ship even though it was close to Christmas. A lot of seamen with A-books hadn't been able to ship out for a long time and were as hungry as I was. I don't remember if any jobs were called out on December 17th but I do remember that I never got to bid on a single one all day. I was feeling pretty depressed by the time I left and went home.

The next day was more of the same. If any jobs were called out, A-books competed with each other and there was no point in even joining the fray. On December 19th, there were no jobs at all and everybody gave up and went home. Half an hour before the hiring hall closed I was the only one there aside from Steve Troy, the union patrolman. A call came in for a Messman/Utility —commonly called a BR—aboard the S.S. Producer, a tanker tied up in Portland, Oregon at Swan Island. I got it. Steve told me the ship had taken an all-Seattle crew earlier in the month when she was at Todd Shipyard, before steaming into the Columbia River several days ago. "I don't know where she's bound but I do know the new owner wants to get under weigh, fast, before the ILWU walks out again and won't cast off lines. Report to the Chief Steward at 0800 tomorrow."

I never figured out exactly what "BR" stands for—maybe bedroom steward—but I do know what he does. The BR makes the officers' beds and cleans their toilets; handles the ship's laundry; and gives out supplies like sheets, towels, soap, etc. to the unlicensed members of the crew. I was more than glad to have a job even though it was probably the worst one on a merchant ship in terms of having to lick boot.

I begged a ride from a friend and got to my new ship on time. She was a T-2 tanker registered in New York, displacing about 10,000 tons of seawater I guessed, built at the end of W.W. II. It looked like the ship had been cut in half and lengthened to maybe 600 feet. She sported quite a bit of rust and looked like a tramp. The "house"—a superstructure with the engine room, living quarters and the bridge—was at the stern. It appeared the ship was carrying a bulk cargo of grain rather than oil. I walked up the gangway with my white duffel bag a few minutes before 0800.

The gangway watchman was about my size—of average height and build—but a bit heavier and with a Van Dyke beard showing traces of gray. I would later learn that he was the Ordinary Seaman on the 8-12 watch; his name was Mike Zubovich, and he was the brother of Steve Troy, the union patrolman. Much later I would learn that he was Mike Costello's "mule" and that he wouldn't return alive from the voyage upon which we were about to embark.

"I'm the new BR." I stood in front of him. "Where's the Steward?" The Ordinary didn't say anything but jerked his thumb toward the stern where the galley was. "Where we headed?" I asked.

"Persian Gulf." The Ordinary finally spoke.

"When're we going to sail?" Getting information out of him was only slightly easier than pulling teeth. He seemed to ponder my question as though it was subject to philosophical debate.

"Couple days," he finally allowed.

"Who owns this rust bucket, anyway?" I persisted.

"Alioto, the mayor of 'Frisco." The Ordinary suddenly got animated. "Look at this!" He held up an old copy of Look magazine. "Alioto's suing Look for $12 million, for bad-mouthing him."

"That might be a tough case to win," I commented. I'd read a little bit in the newspapers about Joseph Alioto's legal problems. He was facing criminal charges of bribery and conspiracy, and was being sued over giving kickbacks to the Washington State Attorney General after getting something like $2 million in legal fees for a case in that state.

"Yeah," the Ordinary agreed. "He got caught with his hand in somebody's pocket. Maybe that's why he's transferring ownership of this tub to his son."

"I'd better turn to," I said, "so I don't get in dutch with the Steward."

"You mean Panama Frank? Fuck that weasely little shit! He's got his nose so far up the Old Man's ass that he probably doesn't even know that the other BR quit. Go stow your gear first. You've got plenty of time to work later."

"O.K., where's my fo'c'sle?" Fo'c'sle, short for forecastle, is a hangover term from days of sail when common sailors slept before the mast.

"Starboard side, aft, one deck down."

"Thanks, man." I hoisted up my duffel bag and walked toward the house. Once I got there, I looked for the Steward's cabin rather than my own fo'c'sle, ignoring the Ordinary's advice. I found it on the main deck, aft of cabins for some Engineers even though the Steward wasn't an officer like they were. The deck level where one slept reflected a pecking order of sorts. The Mates, Radio Operator, and Captain had their cabins on higher decks, and unlicensed seamen slept below the main deck. I soon learned that the Producer carried a complement of 11 officers, licensed by the Coast Guard, and 27 unlicensed seamen.

The door to the Chief Steward's office and cabin was open. Two men were inside, arguing. The Steward was seated at his desk where a cigarette burned in an ashtray. Panama Frank was skinny and balding, with the complexion of a mulatto, and of an indeterminate age between 40 and 60 years. He looked withered somehow and would be lucky to weigh 150 pounds. Towering next to him was a huge black man, well over six feet in height with broad shoulders and weighing upwards of 250 pounds. "Steward, if you don't sign those OT sheets I'm going to break every single finger on the hand you hold a pen with."

Panama Frank's hand trembled as he signed a half-dozen overtime sheets and then handed them to the other man—the 2nd-Cook-and-Baker, called Eddie Jackson, as I soon learned.

"Who are you?" Eddie Jackson demanded to know as he walked out.

"BR. Name's John."

"I'm the union delegate for the Steward Department. Bring your dispatch card to the galley after you're through here," he said as he left.

"New BR, Steward." I handed the Steward half the job dispatch card I'd been given at the union hall. The other half was for the union delegate.

"The officers on here are very demanding, BR, and insist on the best in service. Come with me. I'll show you the linen locker." We went down one level to where the fo'c'sles for most of the unlicensed crew were and walked through a narrow passageway on the port side painted light green and smelling of disinfectant. The small linen locker was at the end past the storerooms for dry and refrigerated food provisions and past a small, empty storeroom. The storeroom was flooded for some reason with water on deck to the level of the combing, a lip about eight inches high at the doorsill.

The only thing Panama Frank explained to me about my new job was that the ship was on a very tight budget and that I should take care not to hand out too many boxes of matches or bars of soap to the unlicensed crew. "The owner doesn't permit overtime except for normal duties on weekends and holidays." He handed me the key for the linen locker.

"OK, Steward. I'm going to go stow my gear." I went to find my fo'c'sle as Panama Frank scurried back up to his cabin.

I crossed over to the starboard passageway and walked aft again. At the end I came to a door stenciled "4 Messmen". The fo'c'sle was painted gray and was large—maybe 15 feet fore-and-aft by 30 feet thwartships (across). There were two double bunks. One set was next to the hull, the outside wall of the ship, between the two portholes. The other set was inboard, at the opposite bulkhead, or inside wall. There were two small writing tables and one sink. Four metal lockers lined the forward bulkhead. All the bunks were made up except for the upper one, inboard. 'Must be mine,' I thought. I went back to the linen locker for sheets and blankets.

After I made my bunk and stowed the contents of my seabag, I went up to the galley to meet the rest of the Steward Department. The galley was on the main deck, at the back of the house and between the seamen's messhall and the saloon, where the officers ate. Forward of the galley, in a thwartship passage between the messhall and the saloon, was a small area for the Pantryman to wash dishes and prepare salads and desserts. From both the messhall and the galley one could walk onto the fantail above the propeller at the very back of the ship.

When I walked into the galley I first noticed stainless steel fixtures against white walls. Huge stoves lined the bulkheads and two long steel counters were in the middle with racks of pots hanging overhead. Panama Frank was standing by a counter, arguing with a balding man in his fifties wearing a white outfit and a long apron. I stood next to them, respectfully, until my presence was noticed. "I'm the new BR," I said to the man in white, extending my right hand.

"What's your name, son?" His grip was less than firm as we shook hands.

"John."

"I'm Jimmy Coker, the Chief Cook. Most people on here call me Mother Coker." He spoke with a soft Southern accent. "I'll help you with anything you need."

"BR," the Steward interrupted, "the First Assistant Engineer wants his room made up." Panama Frank spoke and acted a bit differently than he had an hour before. I caught a waft of alcohol.

"OK, Steward. I'll learn my way around and then get to work. Give me the key to his cabin."

"He said he left his room unlocked, BR. I keep the master key for the officers' cabins."

The Third Cook was a small Filipino man who looked to be in his early 60s. I went over to introduce myself just as he was preparing to mop the galley floor, the final chore to end the morning meal. His name was Pedro. I don't remember a lot about Pedro except that he kept his head down and quietly did his job.

My new roommates—the Crew Messman, Saloon Messman, and the Pantryman—had already finished with breakfast and were gone. I went below to find the utility locker with my cleaning supplies.

The BR's job is the worst on a ship and, at the same time, the best. In port, the only one who has it easier is the Radio Operator who doesn't have to work at all because the radio is not in use. Most of the officers lock their cabins when in port. Since I was

10

apparently not to be trusted with the master key, I didn't have to clean those cabins and could knock off early to go ashore. I'd swab the passageways, clean the few rooms that were unlocked, and be finished for the day by 0930 at the latest. Even after we put to sea, I'd clean the 4-8 cabins before breakfast, and clean the 12-4 cabins when those officers ate chow at 1130 before their watch. That meant I was usually finished for the day by the time I ate lunch. Unlicensed seamen were responsible for cleaning their own fo'c'sles.

On that, my first day, I wanted to make a good impression so I swept and mopped extra carefully. Anyway, there was no reason to hurry and go ashore because I had no money. After making sure the passageways outside the officers' quarters were spotless, I went into the First Engineer's cabin, which was maybe 20-foot square, plus a head. I made the bed, cleaned the sink and shitter, wiped down the shower, swept and mopped. Even doing an extra-good job, I was finished with all my duties before 1030 hours.

Only one of my new roommates was in our fo'c'sle when I returned. The Saloon Messman introduced himself. "Ed Tinsley," he said, sticking out his hand. Ed was a black man with skin the color of milk chocolate. He looked to be somewhere in his thirties and had a ring in his left ear. Shorter than me, he was built like a brick shithouse and reminded me of a Japanese wrestler.

"I'm John the BR," I said, shaking his hand. "Did I make up the right bunk?"

"You got it, BR. You're above the Crew Messman, Kay Hagen. I've got the lower one over here." He pointed at the outboard bunks. "The Pantryman has the top one."

"Where are they?"

"I think Kay Hagen ran ashore. I hope he comes back sober. I don't know where the Kid is. He's probably hiding somewhere, reading a book."

"Where're we headed in the Persian Gulf, Ed?"

"Not sure. I heard Rasty Nasty," Ed said—mutilating the name for Ras Tanura, Saudi Arabia, at the far end of the Persian Gulf—"but everything about this ship keeps changing. I don't know if the new owner even has a buyer for this load of grain, but I do know that he sure as hell wants to get out of here before the longshoremen walk off again." He went to the sink and splashed water on his face. "I'm going to go set up. I'll catch you later, BR."

After Ed Tinsley went up to the saloon, I familiarized myself with all deck levels in the house and checked out storage spaces for the Steward Department. I went up to the messhall a little after 1100 hours.

The Crew Messman was placing silverware on the six tables in the messhall—four settings for each table. Kay Hagen was my height, trim and clean-shaven, and looked to be in his late 40s. His light brown hair was combed back, with a part and had a gleam from hair tonic. The skin on his face was oddly unwrinkled, like it had been preserved in formaldehyde.

"New BR, name's John." I stuck out my right hand. "Looks like I've got the bunk above you."

"Hi." Kay Hagen shook my hand somewhat tentatively, his own hand shaking. He reeked of booze. Deciding that a further introduction could wait until later, I walked to the pantry.

"I'm the new BR," I said. The Pantryman was putting canned peach halves into about ten bowls lined with iceberg lettuce. He was skinny with a bad complexion, maybe 18 or 19 years old. His name was Steve. I always called him 'the Kid', like everyone else did even though he was only a year or two younger than me. "Need a hand?" I asked. The Kid shook his head.

Technically, I was still on duty even though I'd finished my job. Doing someone else's job was overtime but there was no rule against helping out the other Messmen and, in fact, the BR was something of a 'reservist' and supposed to fill in the gaps when the Steward Department was short-handed. I stuck my head around the corner from the pantry into the saloon. "Hey, Ed. Need a hand?"

"I got it covered, BR." Ed Tinsley had all settings ready on the single long table in the saloon. He stood at parade rest with his hands behind his back, waiting for the officers to start filing in at 1130. His saloon looked a lot cleaner than Kay Hagen's messhall.

I decided to have a leisurely meal on company time and walked back to the messhall. I was the first one to arrive for lunch and chose a seat at the aftermost table, facing forward, so I could check out the crew as they came in to eat. Kay Hagen was putting condiments on each of the tables, finishing up his preparation for the meal. His movements were a little smoother than several minutes before and it looked like he was on automatic pilot. 'I'll bet he could do that job blind,' I thought.

An odd mixture of crewmembers showed up for lunch, most of them old enough to be leftovers from World War II. Normally, on sea watches, the blackgang (unlicensed engine room personnel) and deck sailors from the 12-4 watch came in first, eating early so they could relieve the 8-12 watch. After that the day workers (0800-1700) would appear. Last to come in were the 8-12 watchstanders, who'd just been relieved, after they cleaned up for chow. Most of those on the 4-8 watch would be asleep and not eat lunch. The deck and engine departments were on port watches, however, and I couldn't tell what ratings were coming into the messhall.

"Are you gonna eat?" Kay Hagen stood in front of me. His eyes were glazed over and he didn't appear to recognize me from our introduction several minutes before.

"Yeah. Soup and a sandwich, please." He turned toward the galley and walked like he was on stilts. When he came back I grabbed the bowl of soup out of his hand before he spilled it from shaking.

After lunch I took a nap for a couple hours, tired from getting up at an ungodly time that morning for the four-hour drive from Seattle. When I woke up there were still a couple hours to kill before chow. Someone had left a copy of a Portland newspaper in the messhall and I read the whole thing, paying particular attention to international news, since we were about to steam almost halfway around the globe. It seemed we would be traveling past waters more troubled than the ones the Producer was about to leave. Along our route to the Persian Gulf, India and Pakistan were at war over East Pakistan, an area that would later be called Bangladesh. At the mouth of the Persian Gulf, I read that Iranian marines had landed on some islands whose ownership by Iraq was in dispute. Just south of the Persian Gulf, a bunch of sheikdoms had just merged to form what came to be called the United Arab Emirates. In other news: President Nixon took the U.S. dollar off the gold standard, which meant that a greenback wouldn't be worth as much overseas as it was before.

Nixon also announced that he'd visit Red China in February. Meanwhile, 15,000 West Coast longshoremen, striking for the first time in 20 years, had rejected the shipowners' "best offer" and would walk off the docks again sometime after the New Year.

Dinner was much the same as lunch, except that Kay Hagen was in a little better shape than before.

That evening I met the 8-12 Fireman, Chester Tillman. Chester was balding with thick black eyebrows on a prominent brow. I think he had some Indian blood in him. Combined with a jutting jaw, he reminded me of Cro-Magnon Man. He came into our fo'c'sle when the other Messmen knocked off after dinner, shortly after 1800.

It seemed that Chester and Kay Hagen were drinking buddies from way back. "Where did I leave that overcoat?" Kay Hagen asked rhetorically. He and Chester were seated on either side of one of the writing desks. Both had glasses of straight V.O. blended whiskey—on the rocks—in front of them. I was in my bunk, trying to read. Ed Tinsley and the Kid both fled when Chester came into the room.

"It was in '42," Chester responded. We were on the Murmansk run to Russia."

"No it wasn't. It was in '43. I'd remember something like that."

"Oh yeah," Chester countered, "then where's your overcoat?"

16

"The last time I saw it, it was hanging over a chair at a bar in Murmansk. It was 1943. I remember because a Soviet broad was trying to make time with me so she could snatch my overcoat."

"You're full of shit, Hagen. We were at a government recreation center in Murmansk, not a bar. No broad would make a play for you because you were drunk and couldn't get it up. And it was in '42!"

I rolled over and went to sleep while Kay Hagen and Chester kept arguing.

The next day was much like the day before. I don't remember exactly what I did with all my free time. Probably I walked around Swan Island and might have hit Ed Tinsley up for a small loan so I could buy postcards.

We signed foreign articles on December 22nd, took on something like 40,000 gallons of bunkers (fuel oil), and put to sea the following day. Signing foreign articles means you're bound to a ship for the length of the voyage—lasting up to six months for the Producer—whether you like it or not. The Supreme Court ruled a long time ago that the 13th Amendment to the U.S. Constitution—banning slavery by prohibiting involuntary servitude—does not apply to merchant seamen who sign articles of employment. I didn't know where the Producer was going, but it looked like I was going with her.

II

The S.S. Producer slowly rolled as she crossed the Pacific, steaming at 13 knots. At that speed—15 or 16 mph over land—it would take us well over a month to fetch any port in the Persian Gulf. Wooden ships moan and steel ships groan, I've been told. But the rivets on the Producer seemed to creak as she wallowed along. The hum of turbines in the engine room made strange harmony with the slow rhythm of the sea. The main thing I remember about the outbound voyage is boredom. I played a lot of cards with other crewmembers—usually a game called Casino, for small wagers—read several books, and wrote letters. And I spent a lot of time at the rail on the fantail, smoking cigarettes and looking at the horizon, wondering what it was all about.

The weather was great for winter and I recall running into only one bad storm. It was in the middle of the night when the first wave hit us. We must have rolled broadside into a deep trough because I got thrown out of the top bunk. I was having a nightmare about the Producer sinking and was still asleep when I landed on the deck of my fo'c'sle. I don't know how I could have slept through a jolt like that but the next morning Kay Hagan swore he watched me moving my arms and yelling while trying to swim across the floor. Kay held his sides as he told me this, laughing so hard that I thought he was going to puke.

The Kid got seasick during that storm. He'd been fighting nausea ever since we crossed the Columbia Bar after leaving Portland. He blamed his seasickness on having to look at the ocean out the porthole next to his bunk. The Kid asked to switch bunks with me and I gladly agreed.

The Kid and I were the only young guys on the Producer. I think it was his first or second ship. I tried to look out for him but he didn't seem to want to have much to do with me—or anybody else for that matter. The Kid kept to himself and spent most of his free time in his bunk. I got the feeling that he was freaked out just from being on that ship.

My job was a piece of cake. Most of the officers were easygoing and gave me no trouble about how I cleaned their cabins. The exceptions were the Captain and two of the Engineers.

The Captain was named Bergstrom. Eddie Jackson and Ed Tinsley called him "Whistlebritches" and the name stuck. He was short, wore glasses, had black hair, and a high voice. Whistlebritches seemed to be a fan of the picayune and complained frequently to Panama Frank about how I cleaned his stateroom. I had to go back several times for things like a fingerprint on his bathroom mirror or a smudge on brass trim.

The Chief Engineer was overweight to begin with and Ed Tinsley told me he ate like a pig in the saloon. I had to deal with what came out the other end. He took huge shits and used wads of toilet paper. More often than not the toilet was plugged up and I had to use a plunger. I complained to the Steward but it didn't help. The only one superior to the Chief Engineer is the Captain, and I knew that Panama Frank was afraid of Whistlebritches. I tried mounting the toilet plunger atop the Chief Engineer's toilet but he didn't get the hint. He just moved the plunger aside and took another big crap. After that, I tried taking away all the toilet paper. That didn't work either. He just borrowed a roll from one of the other Engineers and then complained to the Steward that I wasn't doing my job. After that, I put a case of toilet paper in the Chief's cabin, next to the door for the head. The Engineer didn't take that hint either and actually seemed to like the idea of stockpiling. He probably thought I was trying to suck up to him after he reported me to the Steward. I next considered getting some Red Hand from the deck department and sealing his toilet seat shut. But the only thing that would get me, I figured, would be an opportunity to talk to the Coast Guard about "misconduct" when we returned to the U.S. I realized that all I could do was pray for constipation.

The officer who gave me the most trouble was the First Assistant Engineer, Harry Lewis. He put little telltale markers in his cabin to check on how thoroughly I was cleaning. Normally, after I got all the cabins in good shape, I still mopped every day but swept only once a week. "BR, the First Assistant says you're not sweeping his cabin." Panama Frank called out loudly, while running after me as I walked rapidly forward in the port passageway on the main deck, carrying my mop bucket. He was chasing me because I'd ignored his call, moments before, when I walked past his office.

"I do sweep his cabin." I figured that wasn't a lie, technically, because I didn't say how often I swept. To myself I thought: 'How does the First know I'm not sweeping?'

"He says he has proof you're not sweeping, BR. I don't want him complaining to the Captain."

"OK, Steward. I'll keep him happy."

The First Assistant was clean-shaven, trim, and bore a slight resemblance to Robert Taylor, the movie star. He smoked a pipe but was very meticulous and never left a mess. I started sweeping the First's cabin every day but the deck was clean and there was rarely anything to push into my dustpan. On the first day of sweeping, the only thing I swept up was a wooden match that was behind a leg of the First's bed. On the second day, I swept a matchstick from behind the same leg of the bed. On the third day, I picked up the matchstick from the same place and mopped but didn't sweep. Nothing was said. Every day after

21

that I'd pick up the matchstick and then mop the First's cabin, without sweeping.

We were almost to Singapore before the First figured out that I wasn't sweeping his cabin every day. "BR, the First Assistant says you're not sweeping his cabin." Panama Frank found me cleaning the cabin of the little Greek Third Mate, one level above the main deck on the port side. "He said he's going to report to the Captain if I don't make you do your job."

'How does the First know I'm not sweeping now?' I thought, silently cursing him. "OK, Steward," I said out loud. "I'll keep him happy."

I started sweeping the First's cabin every day again because I couldn't find another matchstick. "This guy needs to be short-sheeted," I mumbled to myself.

News came over the radio that the West Coast longshoremen resumed their strike on January 17th. Scuttlebutt in the messhall was that we would steam around the Pacific, carrying tramp cargo, until the strike was over.

The mood in the crew grew foul as the voyage dragged on and we didn't know where we were going or how long we'd be gone. It got worse when the booze ran out. Some in the crew had spells so rough that they bordered on DTs. Panama Frank was more bitchy than usual, but no one took him too seriously. Technically,

U.S. merchant ships are supposed to be alcohol-free but that rule is almost universally ignored. From what I saw, alcoholism was rampant. I figured that the only reason gashounds like Kay Hagen and Chester lived as long as they did was due to involuntary sobriety during long foreign voyages, such as the one we were on. Eddie Jackson, the Baker, turned out to be the smartest alcoholic on the ship.

"Want a shot, BR?" I'd just brought my overtime sheet to Eddie one afternoon. Since the 2nd-Cook-and-Baker works odd hours starting in the very early morning, he usually gets his own small fo'c'sle. We were halfway across the Pacific and everyone's alcohol had run out a long time before, or so I thought.

"A shot . . .? What kind of shot?"

"A shot of whiskey," he said, pulling a half-gallon jug of R&R blended Canadian whiskey out of his locker.

I'd never seen Eddie Jackson drunk. He paced himself, it appeared, so I'd probably never seen him completely sober, either. "Sure," I said.

I wasn't offered a second shot, but during the first one the Baker talked a bit about his life. I'm not sure why he took a white boy like me into his confidence. He talked mostly about his sons. They were both football players. One was at the University of Washington and the other might have been playing pro ball—I can't quite remember. I got the feeling that the Baker regretted his life as a seaman and seemed to be living vicariously through his sons.

"Thanks for the drink, Eddie." I got up to leave. "Make sure Kay Hagen and Panama Frank don't find out you've got a jug."

The whole crew seemed to grow surlier as we crossed the dateline en route to Singapore. After an AB (Able Seaman) almost took a swing at Kay Hagen over burnt toast one day during breakfast, I decided that the situation was getting out of control. 'My shipmates would relax more if they could have a drink,' I thought, 'even if we are in the middle of the Pacific Ocean.'

I knew a bit about the fermentation process from having made homebrew. I started making it in high school, and by college I was brewing steadily because it was the only way to afford beer. I went to the storerooms and took inventory. Fresh provisions were long gone. Gathering up as much canned and dried fruit as I could get away with without the loss being noticed, I hid it all in the little flooded storeroom near the linen locker—wearing a pair of rubber boots I'd scrounged from the deck department. There was no reason for anyone to go in there. Then I got a 10-gallon galvanized steel garbage can and lined it with a large plastic bag, putting it under a shelf in the storeroom where I hoped it looked like part of a clean-up process. After that, I 'liberated' two 20-

pound bags of sugar. I threw all the ingredients into the garbage can, hooked up a hose, and filled the can with water.

Sugar, fruit and water will eventually start fermenting by themselves when exposed to air but I wanted to kick-start the process. I normally started batches of homebrew with about an ounce of yeast. The only yeast I could find in the refrigerated storerooms, however, was in "bakers' blocks" of one pound each. 'What the hell,' I thought. 'Let's do this quickly.' The witch's brew splashed up when I threw in a one-pound block.

The fermentation was so robust that by the second day foam overflowed the garbage can. I used a dust pan to regularly scoop it off the surface in the flooded storeroom, worried that someone would notice and wonder why the water on deck had a head on it.

I monitored the brew closely. I could have bottled it before the fermentation stopped and had a carbonated drink that might be called "champagne" ("fruit beer" would have been more accurate). However, I knew from painful experience that one needs to use thick glass when bottling beer or the containers will blow up. The only receptacles available for storing my product were jars for foods such as mayonnaise and pickles, etc., all made of glass that was rather thin. To avoid exploding jars, I needed to let my brew ferment all the way down to "wine" and then seal it off from exposure to air before the wine turned to vinegar.

The brew stopped bubbling after about 10 days and I lined up the empty jars I'd been collecting. Before starting to bottle it, I scooped up a double-handed sample to taste. 'Rotgut wine,' I thought. It was sour and yeasty but the "bouquet" included lots of alcohol. Sugar equals alcohol, in the fermentation process, on a one-to-one basis, but alcohol kills the yeast, and stops fermentation, when it reaches a content of about 15% by volume. I figured my concoction had hit the upper limit for alcohol.

I cut a section of 3/8" hose to siphon the brew into jars at a high-volume flow but estimated I'd need at least an hour of privacy to drain the whole garbage can. I didn't want to attract attention by closing the watertight door that was normally left open, so I waited until supper that evening. In case of unexpected passersby, I set up the bottling operation so that I had my back to the passageway to block sight of the siphon hose and jars, then arranged props of a dustpan and five-gallon bucket to give me a cover story about scooping out the standing water. No one passed the flooded storeroom and all the liquid got into the jars, smooth as silk. I hid them all in the storeroom, washed out and returned the garbage can and other paraphernalia, and went back to my fo'c'sle just as the other Messmen returned from finishing up the evening meal.

The next afternoon I got a pickle jar full of my rotgut wine and offered a taste to my bunkmates. The Kid declined but Ed

Tinsley, the Saloon Messman, grabbed the jar and took a slug. "That tastes like shit, BR, but I'll bet it sure as hell does the trick."

I took the jar and handed it to Kay Hagen. He smelled it, then drank deeply. "Riight!" he sighed. We decided to host a happy hour for the Steward Department that evening.

After supper, our fo'c'sle became Party Central. The Chief Cook and the Third Cook didn't drink, and I can't remember what the Kid did. Panama Frank wasn't invited. We did invite a few unlicensed seamen from other departments. The ones I remember were Chester—Kay's drinking buddy from the Engine Department—and Mike Zubovich, 8-12 Ordinary from the Deck Department. Everybody had a good time. Zubovich, the gangway watchman when I first came aboard, told us that he'd killed a man in a Houston bar. He was almost bragging about it. He said that the only reason he was on the Producer was to get money to pay his Texas lawyer for getting the murder charge reduced to a misdemeanor.

The party wound down and everybody left. Everybody except Chester, that is. He and Kay Hagen had opened quite a few jars of my rotgut wine and were at their regular seats on either side of a writing table. "Where'd I leave my overcoat?" Kay Hagen asked Chester. "You were with me on the run to Murmansk. That's the last time I saw it."

27

'Oh, Christ,' I thought, climbing up to my bunk.

"You gave it away to a Russian broad, Hagen. You wanted to fuck her but you couldn't get it up. That's what happened."

I rolled over and went to sleep.

The next morning I had to yell at Kay Hagen before he'd get out of bed to work breakfast. From the empty jars scattered about, it looked like he and Chester had stayed up and gone through another gallon of rotgut after the party was over. I'd made the mistake of telling Kay where I'd made the foul brew. I moved the jars that morning, hiding them in a different part of the flooded storeroom.

It didn't work. Kay found the stash of "wine". The next day he and Chester got shit-faced drunk after lunch. I found Kay passed out in his bunk at 1600 hours. "Kay," I yelled at him, "you've got to go set up for supper!" No response. "Get up, goddammit!" I shook him hard. I might just as well as have been shaking a rag doll because he didn't move when I let go. I realized that I had to serve supper to the crew. "You're going to pay for this, Hagen," I yelled over my shoulder as I left the fo'c'sle to go to the messhall.

It wasn't the first time I'd pulled Kay Hagen's job, and it wouldn't be the last. I never wrote down overtime for doing it because I didn't want Kay to have to sign his name in Whistlebritches' logbook under a description of his misdeeds.

Anyway, doing the Crew Messman's job was like taking a walk in the park. The Cooks were all easy to work with and there were only a few assholes in the crew. Supper was served between 1700 and 1800 and everybody ate early. By 1800 I'd broken down the tables, swept and mopped, and was back in my fo'c'sle.

We were close to the Equator, where the sun rose and set at about 0600 and 1800—six o'clock, AM and PM, to landlubbers —even though it was mid-January. Through the forward porthole I saw the sun sitting on the western horizon. Kay Hagen was still unconscious.

"Kay, get up!" I shook him violently in his bunk until I saw his eyes open. "You've got to go set up for breakfast."

Kay Hagen blinked unbelievingly at me and then looked out the porthole, where the sun was bisected by the horizon. Then he looked at his wristwatch, which read 6:05. Ed Tinsley and the Kid had returned to our fo'c'sle in the meantime and watched with amazement as Kay lurched out of his bunk and went to his locker for a clean white Messman's jacket. He walked unsteadily to the sink and tried to wake up by splashing several handfuls of water on his face then combed his hair and stumbled out of our fo'c'sle toward the messhall.

The next day we heard from the deck department what happened. Pasquale, an AB on the 8-12, walked into the messhall to get a cup of coffee. Kay had tablecloths and silverware on all the tables and was getting glasses from the pantry. "Hagen, what the hell are you doing?" Pasquale asked.

Meanwhile, I told Ed Tinsley and the Kid how I'd settled the score with Kay Hagen. When he returned from the messhall he was met with peals of laughter from all three of us. Kay was plenty pissed off but he was so grateful he didn't have to work breakfast that he didn't do anything about it and dove onto his bunk instead, where he promptly returned to unconsciousness.

Thanks to Pasquale, the word was out that Kay Hagen was drunk in the messhall and had somehow gotten hold of booze in the middle of the ocean. I got nervous that my brewing project would be revealed so I moved the remaining jars of rotgut wine to a new hiding place. I can't remember where I put it but do remember that Kay Hagen and Chester never found it.

We were still several days from Singapore. I rationed the remaining jars of wine to last until then. Mike Zubovich and Chester became regular visitors every evening for an abbreviated happy hour. Zubovich, the 8-12 Ordinary, liked to talk like a tough guy because he'd killed that man in a bar fight. He'd say, 'I'll kill you if you don't do this,' or 'I'll kill you if you don't do that.' Zubovich was no bigger than me and I didn't take him seriously. I didn't know whether he'd killed a man or not and thought that all his talk was bluff and bullshit.

On January 19th, the S.S. Producer moored offshore in Singapore, out in the harbor. We were only there for about 12 hours to take on fuel. Bumboats swarmed around the ship at anchor, and enterprising Chinese threw up grappling hooks to scramble aboard. They brought alcohol, women, and souvenirs— all for sale.

I took a launch ashore with Kay Hagen after lunch and went on a short rickshaw tour. All I remember is a teeming and bustling city. It was wide-open, in terms of vice, and anything was available—for a price; a far cry from the strait-laced place I'm told that Singapore is today.

When we got back to the ship in time for Kay to set up for supper, Panama Frank cornered me. "The First Assistant said you didn't clean his room today, BR."

"His cabin was locked."

"He unlocked it after he ate lunch."

"I was ashore by then, Steward."

"It was still your work hours. The First Assistant says he's going to the Captain if I don't make you do your job."

"OK, Steward, I'll take care of him."

The next morning, after we'd left Singapore, I stripped the First Assistant's bed. I'd once worked as houseboy in a resort hotel and learned a lot from the chambermaids, including how to deal with problem guests. I replaced the linen with one sheet

31

instead of two. Tucking the sheet under the mattress at the head of the bed, I spread it halfway down and then folded it back, forming a pocket in the middle of the bed. I then spread the blanket, folded the sheet over the blanket, and replaced the pillow. After that I swept and mopped.

The next morning the shit hit the fan. "BR, the First Assistant says you aren't making his bed correctly." Panama Frank held up a bed sheet that was almost ripped in half.

"Steward, I don't know how someone can poke their feet through a sheet without using incredible force." I pointed at the shredded sheet. "The First must have been plenty drunk to do this." Panama Frank nodded, knowingly. I never heard another thing about it.

The First Assistant and I entered into something of an unspoken compromise after that episode. I swept his floor every other day, rather than once a week, and he stopped complaining about me to the Steward.

III

The S.S. Producer steamed into the Indian Ocean.

"Iran. That's where we're going," Ed Tinsley announced a couple days after we left Singapore. The Messmen had just returned to our fo'c'sle after finishing up the evening meal. Ed was the best source of scuttlebutt from eavesdropping on the officers eating in the saloon.

"Where in Iran?" Kay Hagen asked.

"Bandar Abbas."

"Never been there," Kay said. "Hell, I've never even heard of it! Where is it?"

"It's at the mouth of the Persian Gulf, where it empties out to the Gulf of Oman and the Arabian Sea. I heard the Chief Mate say that no other American merchant ship ever put in there before. None of the officers know anything about Bandar Abbas."

It took us about two weeks from Singapore to steam across the Indian Ocean and Arabian Sea to the Gulf of Oman. Bandar Abbas was in the Strait of Hormuz, which links the Persian Gulf to the Gulf of Oman. We fetched Bandar Abbas the beginning of February 1972. Whistlebritches restricted us to the ship and we couldn't go ashore because, he said, the local authorities didn't want us to.

We'd been at sea for over 40 days and the crew was half-crazed to walk on land. The SIU contract has a section about unlicensed seamen being entitled to overtime in port when restricted to ship, except during war or by order of the port authorities in cases of emergency. The Steward Department, at least, didn't figure there was any 'emergency' and claimed that

Whistlebritches needed to be more forceful about demanding that we be let ashore. We started writing down 24 hours per day on our overtime sheets. Panama Frank had a fit.

I went out on deck to look around shortly after we tied up. Ed Tinsley told me that temperatures could hit 135 Fahrenheit in the Persian Gulf but that day it felt like a mild 80 degrees. Bandar Abbas was flat, barren and desert-like. It looked like a shit-ass fishing village that recently had an industrial port laid on top of it. We were docked at a wharf that looked brand-new but had no cranes or other machinery to unload our cargo of grain. Just beyond the foot of the wharf were parked a couple dozen Mercedes dump trucks that also looked brand-new. A small army of half-naked Iranian workers filed aboard, headed for the holds. Hans Lee, the Bo's'n, was leading a few of his sailors past me to work cargo. I went back in the house so I wouldn't get in the way.

That afternoon I was back out on deck to watch the cargo operation. The deck department was using ropes and winches to pull up nets out of the holds. In each net was a pallet stacked six or seven feet high with cotton sacks full of grain. The nets were swung outboard to the wharf with a boom and lowered onto old dilapidated trucks. I wondered why the new Mercedes trucks sat idle. I went to No. 1 Hatch—the hold nearest the house—lit a cigarette and leaned over the raised lip to watch the Iranian longshoremen in action. At least 20 of them were down in the hold, each scooping grain into a sack and then stacking the sack onto a pallet. 'An unloading process like that is going to take a while,' I thought. In fact, it took 17 days.

The Iranian workers spent all day in the holds and ate there as well. They were allowed to come up at night to sleep on deck. They weren't allowed in the house and I wondered how they took care of other bodily functions. I found out later, when going back out on the main deck for another episode of longshore theatre. One of the Iranians in the hold walked over to the forward corner on the starboard side, squatted down and took a crap. While he was hitching up his pants, his mate came along, scooped up the grain behind him and put it into a sack, turds and all. He then topped off his sack, sealed it, and stacked it on the pallet. 'I've got to remember not to eat any bread while I'm here,' I thought as I went back inside.

The first day we were in Bandar Abbas, an Iranian merchant sneaked aboard with fifths of Johnnie Walker scotch, Red Label. While selling the bottles for exorbitant prices, the man made excuses about why the seals on the caps were broken, babbling some strange explanation involving customs inspectors and about alcohol not being allowed in Moslem countries. The story didn't make much sense to me but several others in the crew, including Kay Hagen and Chester, bought all he brought aboard.

"Come on, BR," Chester said that evening when he was in our fo'c'sle, "have a drink. Don't be a pussy." He was sitting at one of the writing desks with Kay Hagen, a fifth of Johnnie Walker standing between them. I finally agreed to half a water glassful on the rocks. It tasted funny and had a strange bite to it. I started feeling bad and went to bed while Kay and Chester argued over the last known location of Kay's overcoat in Murmansk.

I don't know what was in that "scotch" but I couldn't sleep and it sure made my stomach churn. Kay Hagen called it "gasoline" but he and Chester kept throwing it down. I lay in my bunk feeling worse and worse.

"I'm going to kill you." I was jerked out of a half-sleep to see Chester standing next to my bunk, his face a few inches from mine. His eyes were totally bloodshot, with pupils that looked like they were balls in a pinball machine.

"Why, Chester?" I looked past him. The fifth of Johnnie Walker was empty and Kay Hagen lay unconscious on his bunk. The Kid was asleep on the bunk above him.

"Because you're the BR and I'm the mayor of Capitol Hill." I'd heard Chester claim to be the mayor of Seattle's Capitol Hill before. I'd once lived in an apartment on Capitol Hill when I started at the University of Washington. As far as I knew it was

36

still a neighborhood, rather than a city, so I'm not sure where Chester obtained his title.

"You're drunk, Chester, and I feel like shit. Kill me tomorrow." I moved my left foot from under the cover, put it on Chester's chest and pushed him firmly toward the door.

"I'm not going to forget this." Chester said as he staggered out of the fo'c'sle. "I'll get you, BR."

I fell into a restless sleep, troubled by nightmares. The worst one had the Producer spinning around in a whirlpool, with me the only one aboard. I bolted upright—forced awake by vomit rising in my throat—and only barely got my mouth past the edge of the bunk before puking my guts out. Dry heaves started when there was nothing left in my stomach. Ed Tinsley kept his slippers on the deck by the side of his bunk. While I leaned over the side of my bunk, retching and gagging, I saw to my horror that his right slipper was filled with vomit. I didn't think Chester was able to kill me but I knew that Ed Tinsley was. I didn't care. Being dead would probably feel better. When the dry heaves finally stopped I fell into a state better described as toxic shock than sleep.

Ed Tinsley had a morning drill where every movement was the same. As soon as we were called at 0600 by the deck watch, Ed would raise his knees from the bedspread, rock back and swing his legs out of bed. He'd then rock forward as part of a continuous movement, sitting upright as both feet simultaneously slid into his slippers in the exact spot where he left them every night. That morning at 0600, when the AB on gangway watch called us to turn-to, I lay in my bunk waiting in dread while I felt Ed rock back and then rock forward again as he swung his legs out of bed to his slippers.

"Motherfucker . . . . BR!!!"

I didn't say anything. Ed sprang up, his face twisted with homicidal intent. I almost hoped he'd put me out of my misery.

"Oh, BR . . . ." His look changed to one of disgust. "You're fucked up."

Lucky for me that we were in port and I didn't have any cabins to clean. By lunchtime I was able to keep down a bowl of broth that I begged from Mother Coker. After that I went through the motions of cleaning the passageways, making sure that Panama Frank saw me.

The counterfeit scotch didn't seem to affect Kay Hagan and Chester like it did me. I'm not sure about others in the crew. The only one I remember is Koons, the 4-8 Fireman. He had to sign the logbook because he couldn't stand his watch after the "scotch" was brought aboard. A few days later, an Oiler named John Buckley tripped over a combing while going into the engine room and broke his arm near the shoulder. I'm not sure whether alcohol was involved or not.

After a couple of days we were finally allowed to go ashore. It was in the late afternoon, shortly before dusk, when a bunch of us got to the security gate. We had to argue with the Iranian guards over whether or not seaman's papers—a Merchant Mariner's Document—was sufficient identification to leave the ship because no one had a passport. After getting past the guards we immediately tried to find a bar.

Alcohol is prohibited in Iran, I was told, but concessions were made to foreign workers. We ended up at a place in the desert, a short taxi ride away, that was a large, single-story cinderblock building crowded with Westerners. From the accents, I guessed that a goodly number of those present were English and Scot. On the wall facing the long bar was a larger-than-life portrait of Shah Reza Pahlavi in military uniform, leveling a steely gaze at the patrons below.

Separating myself from my shipmates, I squeezed through the crowd and bellied up to the bar. Before ordering a drink, I turned to the guy on my left, a middle-aged fellow with a bit of a potbelly and going bald. I assumed he was from England. "Sir, I had a bad experience with alcohol in this country. Can you vouch for the purity of the drinks in this establishment?"

"Son, you're safe having any drink you want," he answered in a Texas drawl, "and I'll buy you the first one of whatever it is.

What's a young Yankee like you doing in the middle of the desert?"

"Merchant seaman. S.S. Producer. How about you?" I ordered a capped bottle of beer, still slightly nervous about broken seals on bottles of hard liquor.

The Texan worked for an American oil corporation that was part of a consortium of Western oil companies. He said he was in the process of helping to develop Bandar Abbas into the largest port in Iran for the export of oil.

"What was here before development started?" I asked.

"Nothing. I heard the Shah used it as a penal colony for his political enemies. 10 or 15 years ago no one lived here except a handful of fishermen."

"What's the rest of Iran like?" I asked as the Iranian bartender brought me my beer.

"I've only been to Tehran, the capital," the Texan said. "The Shah is trying to modernize this country but I doubt he'll have much luck outside Tehran. Ragheads are real religious and don't like change. The Shah can hang on to power thanks to his secret police, the SAVAK, but as soon as you leave the capital the mullahs call the shots. I heard that a woman visiting here from Tehran last week got whipped in public for wearing a short skirt and no veil."

I heard Chester's voice as I took a slug of beer. He was a few feet to my right, in front of the portrait of the Shah, drinking doubles and talking loudly to someone next to him.

"I saw a fleet of Mercedes trucks near the wharf we're tied to," I said to the oilman from Texas. "Why aren't they being used to carry our grain?"

"The Shah got a bunch of trucks from the Krauts, traded for oil, but he didn't get any mechanics or spare parts to go with them. These sandniggers have a lot of money but they don't know shit. The trucks probably stopped running because of some sand in the air filters and there's no one that can change 'em." Just then there was a loud crack to the right of us, from a glass being slammed down hard. It was Chester.

"Fuck the Shah!" Chester shouted. He had stepped back and was holding his right arm out stiffly, sticking up his middle finger at the portrait behind the bar. The place became deathly quiet.

I wanted to get out of there, fast! At the wall to my right, beyond the end of the bar, was an outside door. The bar itself was about four feet high and the top of it extended outward toward customers a couple feet, like a shelf, leaving an open space underneath. I didn't say goodbye to the Texan, and instead bent over in a crouch and ran under the shelf of the bar, bruising thighs with my shoulder as I tunneled my way past numerous legs on the way to the door. It was no time to be polite. There was still a stunned silence when I got to the end. I burst through the door and, once outside, ran through the desert as fast as I could.

I didn't see anybody chasing me and slowed down when I was out of breath. The new moon was barely a sliver as I walked under a starry sky. After I found the waterfront, I figured it was only a matter of following the shoreline until I got to my ship. On the way, I passed fishing boats and a couple of military launches that looked like P.T. boats.

A bit farther, I finally caught sight of the Producer's lights in the distance. A few yards in front of me I saw a large pit, three or four feet deep, that could have been an excavation for a new building. At the same time I heard, or felt, a rumbling just ahead and squinted into the darkness.

'Holy shit!' A platoon of soldiers in full battle dress was running toward me. I dove head-first into the pit. Dozens of combat boots loudly passed at double time as I crouched down, shaking with fear. 'Chester's done it this time,' I thought. 'There're enough troops to arrest the whole crew.'

I stayed in the hole until the soldiers disappeared into the darkness, then warily resumed my trek. The guards at the security gate didn't challenge me and I safely made it back to the ship.

Chester was brought back by the local authorities later that night. I heard the next day that Iran had sent more marines in boats to nearby islands at the mouth of the Persian Gulf, strengthening its claim against Iraq over who exactly owned them.

To attract and keep foreign workers, the government made "white"—that is, non-Arabic and non-Persian— prostitutes available. They were at the "Compound," a walled village out in the desert that had women and alcohol for the asking—at steep prices. The Compound became the destination of choice for my shipmates. I went once. In addition to the high prices, the women—mostly from countries in Eastern Europe—seemed to be there against their will and I didn't have much fun. Mike Zubovich, on the other hand, had so much fun that he stayed at the Compound for days on end. I don't know where he got the money to do that because Ordinary Seamen were paid only a few dollars more per month than Messmen.

Money became a problem. In addition to my one visit to the Compound and a few more visits to the bar where Chester might have gotten us executed, I bought a lot of souvenirs. Bandar Abbas had a bustling bazaar in the old part of town. Persian rugs, hookahs and other items were available at prices cheaper than those my shipmates were paying to longshoremen and other vendors who came aboard the Producer. After several days I was broke. The SIU contract had a provision that unlicensed seamen are allowed to draw against their wages once every five days while vessels are in port. But draws are allowed only from base wages, not from overtime pay—a significant portion of my earnings—and the whole time we were in Bandar Abbas I was allowed to draw a total of only $200. I couldn't stretch out the meager draws for five days at a time.

With no money, I started wandering around Bandar Abbas in the afternoons. I can't remember much about what the village looked like other than a lingering impression of tent-slums in the desert. Ninety percent of the inhabitants seemed to live in filth and poverty. I do remember the stares I got when I wandered beyond the immediate vicinity of the port where it got even more barren and desert-like. The reaction to my blue eyes and ruddy complexion made it obvious that the inhabitants had never seen a person with light skin before. I traded a pack of chewing gum to an Iranian kid for lessons in counting up to 1,000 in Farzi, the Persian language.

The next time the crew got a draw I returned to the bazaar, armed with my new ability with the Farzi number system. I soon discovered that in addition to the price first quoted, there was a 'second price' and a 'third price' as well as a 'last price'. I bartered for the souvenirs that my shipmates wanted—hookahs were the most popular—and resold them on the ship for 'second price' at a considerable profit. My mates were still saving money because they had been paying 'first price' or more. I no longer had to worry about being broke in that port.

While we were in the desert heat of Bandar Abbas, northern Iran was having one of the worst winters on record. The mountains it shared with southern Afghanistan saw the heaviest snowstorm in a century. I would later learn that Mike Costello was trapped on the Tarzian Pass in northern Iran with 40 kilos of hash, trying desperately to get to the S.S. Producer before she sailed away.

Meanwhile, John Buckley the Oiler was still on board, with a broken arm that was getting worse. There were precious few medical facilities in Bandar Abbas. Those that were there left something to be desired and Whistlebritches couldn't get the Iranians to issue travel documents to send Buckley back to the U.S. Ed Tinsley heard someone in the saloon say "gangrene".

Mike Zubovich, the Ordinary, proclaimed himself 'King of the Compound' and only came back to the ship occasionally. I don't know how he arranged for his watch partners to cover for him or if they did. Zubovich was on the 8-12 watch. I heard he had words with Pete Ahearn, an AB on the 4-8 watch, over Zubovich not relieving Pete as gangway watchman. Pete Ahearn was an ex-Marine—from the Korean War era, I guessed. He was tall and lean, clean-shaven with a square jaw. He was a head taller than Mike Zubovich and in a lot better shape. I doubt that Pete ever went to the Compound. When Pete confronted Zubovich about all the times he hadn't been relieved from gangway watch, Zubovich said, "Shut up or I'll kill you." It turned out that Pete took the comment literally.

There was also some funny business, while we were in Bandar Abbas, about who really owned the S.S. Producer. Letters that trickled in from home came in care of "Freighters, Inc."—whatever that meant. Alioto's son—I can't remember his name—showed up, came aboard, and said that he owned the ship. I didn't actually meet the man but did see him touring the passageways with Whistlebritches and Panama Frank. Alioto Jr. complained about the amount of overtime paid to the crew, spots on the walls, and other piss ant problems—never mind that the Oiler, John Buckley, couldn't get medical attention and was knocking on heaven's door.

Mountain roads connecting Afghanistan to Iran were paralyzed with snow. Mike Costello got through, somehow, and made it to Bandar Abbas. I don't know how he bullshitted his way past the security gate, but he showed up on the gangway a day or two before we sailed for Singapore. I had only passing contact with Mike in Bandar Abbas when he came through the messhall with his cases of soda. He was tall—maybe 6'5"—and barrel-chested, in his mid-twenties. Mike was a merchant seaman and had no trouble finding his way around a T-2 tanker like the Producer. He had a twinkle in his eye and a ready smile. And he was very persuasive, as I would later learn first-hand. After selling the soda for a tidy profit, he made a deal with Whistlebritches to take Buckley to Tehran for transport to medical attention in the U.S.—offering to do what Whistlebritches and Alioto, Jr. were evidently incapable of arranging. Whistlebritches gave Mike a small fortune for expenses and bribes, and maybe—I'm not sure about this—the promise of a job back to the U.S. on the Producer.

The S.S. Producer cast off the 20th of February and left Bandar Abbas in ballast—with no cargo—other than 40 kilos of hashish hidden somewhere aboard. Ed Tinsley said we were bound for Singapore for fuel, and no one knew where we were going after that. There was scuttlebutt about turning south to pick up a load of ore in East Africa and take it either to New Jersey or the Gulf of Mexico where the longshoremen were not on strike. Right after that we got word that the West Coast longshore strike settled the same day we left Bandar Abbas. That meant we could go back to the U.S. instead of tramping around for cargo. Then the scuttlebutt was that we were to go to San Francisco for repairs before steaming to Sacramento for a load of rice. Rumor had it that Alioto Sr. was the head of some 'Rice Commission' and would profit handsomely if the rice were delivered to Korea or to some other nation, perhaps in the Mediterranean. At the time, the Producer was in the Arabian Sea, almost to the Indian Ocean.

IV

It happened on February 27, 1972, a Sunday. I remember because there was no moon that night. I guess the killer planned it that way so he wouldn't be seen from the bridge. Pete Ahearn, one of the 4-8 ABs, got relieved of wheel watch on the bridge by the 4-8 Ordinary at 1935 hours and went to relieve the other 4-8 AB, Don Howard, for the last 20 minutes of look-out on the bow.

Each of the three deck watches had two ABs and an Ordinary Seaman. During the day, one sailor would be at the wheel steering the ship, with the other two working on deck. After dark, in addition to the sailor at the wheel on the bridge, one stood look-out and the other sailor was on stand-by—making coffee, calling the next watch, and generally killing time in the messhall in case the officer on the bridge called down for something. The three would rotate duties, with each man spending an hour and twenty minutes at each task during the four-hour watch. The 4-8 split the evening watch segments—one hour and 20 minutes each—into parts so everybody could eat

48

supper. Pete had it figured when he'd have the last look-out on the 4-8 and Zubovich would have the first one on the 8-12, a time when the two would be in the same place with no witnesses.

At about 1955 hours, Mike Zubovich, the 8-12 Ordinary, left the messhall and walked forward on the main deck. From the house he passed the hatch covers to holds 1 through 6, numbered from stern to bow. He likely walked slowly, in no hurry to relieve the 4-8 AB on time. Zubovich was dressed for balmy weather—in a T-shirt, shorts and open-toed shower shoes—but carried a navy-blue hooded sweater in case of chill. He also carried a flashlight and transistor radio. Zubovich thought he'd be relieving Pete Ahearn as look-out on the bow. But Pete wasn't waiting on the bow.

Pete would later testify in court that after he and Zubovich had words about the gangway watch in Bandar Abbas and about Zubovich's threats, he sneaked down at night to the machine shop in the engine room to fashion a weapon. He started with a foot-long bolt, one inch in diameter, and began shaping one end with the grinding wheel on one of the workbenches. It took him two nights because he turned off the grinding wheel and hid whenever an Oiler or an Engineer walked by. He ground the bolt to a cylindrical point, like the bottom of an ice cream cone. Next he cut the head off a mop and lashed the pointed bolt to the end of the handle. Pete hid the jury-rigged spear under his mattress and waited for the perfect night to take care of Mike Zubovich.

The look-out stands on the prow, the forwardmost part of the bow that sticks out over the ocean. Just before 1955 hours, Pete left his post on the prow and hid behind the anchor windlass—a machine with large horizontal drums used to bring the anchor chains up and to tension mooring lines—just forward of No. 6 Hatch. As Zubovich approached the bow he didn't see anyone to relieve and started looking around. Pete sprang out from behind the windlass with his spear.

From later looking at the body and from testimony in court, I think I can put together what happened next: Pete Ahearn started thrusting at Mike Zubovich with the homemade spear. "What the fuck!" The Ordinary dropped his flashlight and parried with his arms as the AB poked with the spear. Zubovich got a hole in his left forearm and couldn't block a puncture wound to his left hip. "You're nuts . . . !" The AB grimly kept jabbing and jabbing, without saying a word. He got through the Ordinary's defenses and, all of a sudden, Zubovich had a hole in his lower left lung. At that point the Ordinary bolted out of his shower shoes and started running aft toward the house, with the AB chasing him. Witnesses in the crew would later testify that the Ordinary's sweater and flashlight were found near the anchor windlass. Next to No. 6 Hatch was a broken transistor radio.

Pete was maybe five inches taller than Zubovich, with longer legs and in a lot better shape. The Ordinary ran the best 100-yard dash of his life. I don't know how he did it, especially with only one lung working, but Zubovich outran Pete Ahearn over the length of the main deck. Pete gave up the chase when Zubovich was close to the house. He'd failed to pull off the perfect murder and threw his spear into the ocean.

Outrunning Pete with a few holes in his body had taken a toll on Zubovich. When he got inside the house and realized he was no longer being pursued, Zubovich slowed down and stumbled along the port side passageway, leaving bloody handprints on the bulkhead. "Ahearn has gone mad. He just stabbed me," Zubovich said when he got to the messhall. Don Howard, AB on the 4-8, and Pasquale—8-12 AB on standby—were in the messhall bullshitting with the Bo's'n, Hans Lee. Zubovich was bleeding badly from several places. He staggered through the messhall, using the tables for support, and went out to the fantail, where he collapsed.

I was sitting at a desk in my fo'c'sle writing a letter to one of my sisters when the Baker, Eddie Jackson, came in. "Someone's hurt, BR. Bring some blankets up to the fantail, now!" I did as he said without asking questions.

When I got to the fantail, carrying a half-dozen blankets, about six of the crew stood in a circle gawking at the Ordinary lying in a pool of blood. I pushed past my shipmates and knelt next to him. Zubovich was lying on his back about six feet from the port rail, his head toward the bow, gasping for air. "Are you OK, Mike?" With all the blood on him, I realized how ridiculous my question was as soon as the words left my mouth. I put a blanket over his stomach and legs, while wondering how a blanket was going to help. The Ordinary's chest was heaving and it sounded like he was trying to breathe under water, blood gurgling out of the wound with every breath.

"I can't breathe." Those were Mike Zubovich's last words. I watched a shadow pass over his face. It was like the gray light during a partial eclipse of the sun. I'd never watched a man die before, but I knew he was dead. The Chief Mate, Mr. Marz, arrived and tried to administer oxygen through a mask but the dead man would have none of it.

Meanwhile, the Bo's'n went to notify the Captain. As later related by Hans Lee, Whistlebritches had locked the door and initially refused to come out of his stateroom. "There's a man dying on deck, Captain!" The Bo's'n pounded on the door. Whistlebritches must have feared a mutiny because, when he finally came out, he was carrying a .45 semi-automatic pistol. He likely thought that Hans Lee was trying to trick him into coming onto the main deck so the unlicensed crew could jump him. Firearms are forbidden on U.S. merchant ships. I was told that there is an exception for the Captain to have a gun—perhaps for the very reason he thought he needed one that night.

When Whistlebritches finally got to the fantail, the .45 strapped to his waist, what was left of Mike Zubovich was growing cold. I was still kneeling next to him, folding my blankets. A few of the crew remained on the fantail, talking quietly at the very stern, by the mast for the flag. Whistlebritches tried to walk with a swagger but he was obviously nervous. He pulled a small rectangular mirror out of his breast pocket, bent over, and put it under the Ordinary's nose. "He's not dead," Whistlebritches announced, imagining he saw vapor on the mirror from the dead man's breath. If I had any respect remaining for the Captain of my ship, there was none left after he said that. Hans Lee told a couple of the ABs to take Zubovich's body to the refrigerated meat locker beneath the galley.

While all this was happening on the fantail, Pete Ahearn sat in the messhall, mere yards away, drinking coffee. He was as cool as a cucumber and didn't say a word.

There was a spare mate's cabin one level above the main deck on the port side. After bars were hastily welded across the porthole, Pete was put in irons and placed there. I can't remember whether the steel shackles were around his ankles, his wrists, or both.

We were only a few days away from Singapore but the voyage there was painful. The Kid acted funny. Ed Tinsley was OK, but Kay Hagen drank too much. He'd stockpiled booze in Bandar Abbas and got so drunk that I had to serve supper for him a couple of times. The little Greek Third Mate, I think Korinis was his name, freaked out about being in the cabin next to a murderer. I don't know how he thought that Pete was going to get through the steel bulkhead that separated them but the Third Mate refused to stay in his cabin, and instead slept on the settee in the cabin for the other Third Mate. Ed Tinsley said Korinis was so nervous that he was going to the medical officer for Phenobarbital on a regular basis. I had a nightmare that Mother Coker pulled the wrong entrée from the meat locker and served Mike Zubovich for chow. Whistlebritches hid in his stateroom and Panama Frank hid in his cabin. Panama Frank came out only once that I know of. He told me that the Captain complained that I'd missed a spot of blood on the bulkhead when I cleaned the port passageway on the main deck.

The Bo's'n, Hans Lee, was assigned to stand Mike Zubovich's 8-12 watch. The Day Man (Deck Maintenance AB working 0800-1700), Jack Ryan, was assigned to stand Pete Ahearn's 4-8 watch. In the Engine Department Bill Hatchell, Engine Utility (another day worker), had been standing John Buckley's watch as Oiler since Bandar Abbas.

The U.S. Coast Guard came aboard when we anchored out in the harbor off Singapore on March 3rd. Singapore had become an independent nation a few years before and I didn't understand how or why a branch of the U.S. military was stationed there. Nevertheless, several Coast Guard officers and enlisted personnel in starched white uniforms convened a meeting with the crew in the messhall. We were told that both the killer and the dead man had to be carried back to the U.S. on the Producer. That meant another four weeks with a prisoner and a corpse. Neither the Captain nor the Steward chose to attend the meeting. I got pissed off. 'A Coast Guard pencil-pusher of a Lieutenant in a pansy-assed uniform is explaining footnotes in the Code of Federal Regulations,' I was thinking, 'while my shipmates are going nuts.'

"Sir, why is it that a murderer and a dead man can't be taken off here, sir?" The unlicensed crew grumbled loudly in agreement with my question.

The Lieutenant spoke in bureaucratese and spouted some song-and-dance about transportation not being available.

"I don't understand, sir. Planes from America fly here all the time. I'll bet that's how you got here and that's how you'll leave. Are you saying there's only room for you?"

The Lieutenant changed the subject. My shipmates in the messhall, however, were muttering obscenities, and I suspect the Lieutenant got nervous about whether he and his contingent would have trouble leaving the ship. The Lieutenant made a compromise whereby the corpse would be taken off the ship, but we'd have to carry the killer to the authorities in San Francisco.

The little Greek Third Mate, Korinis, refused to stay on the ship with Pete Ahearn aboard but changed his mind about getting off in Singapore when told that he'd be charged with desertion. The American Consul in Singapore, a guy named Coffey, had come aboard with the Coast Guard and persuaded or coerced Korinis not to jeopardize his Coast Guard license—to say nothing of his freedom.

A launch carrying the ship's agent came alongside as the meeting with the Coast Guard wound down. The agent scrambled aboard. Right behind him, coming up the gangway from the same launch, was Mike Costello.

Years later, while sitting in a Seattle bar, Mike told me how he got there and what happened after he came aboard. "I took a plane with Buckley to Shiraz, Iran, then continued on to Tehran to put him into a hospital and await transport to the States. From Tehran, I went back to Afghanistan to get more hash.

"I strapped 10 kilos to my body," Mike said matter-of-factly, "in flat bricks of one kilo each. Getting to Singapore was more difficult than I expected. D. B. Cooper hijacked that flight to Portland just three months before and authorities in some countries were worried that he was going to start a fad. I almost got searched in Pakistan, after traveling overland from Afghanistan, when I was boarding a flight to Bangkok. Officials in Thailand and Singapore were still pretty relaxed and I had no more trouble.

"I didn't know Zubovich had been killed until I got to the ship.

"The Old Man (Captain) owed me for taking care of Buckley. I told him I was broke and needed to get back to the States. He signed me on as Wiper. As soon as I left the Old Man's stateroom I went below to try to find the 40 kilos I'd given to Zubovich. I didn't have to look far because it was under his bunk in the fo'c'sle for the 8-12 deck watch. That stupid son-of-a-bitch didn't even hide it!

"As soon as I picked up the hash, I heard voices in the passageway, getting closer. The Bo's'n and Bill O'Connor, the deck delegate, were bringing a couple of Coast Guardsmen to get Zubovich's gear. I panicked and threw all 40 kilos out the porthole. I went through the head, just as the door opened, and slipped out the next fo'c'sle."

Mike was the new Wiper, a day worker and the lowest rating in the engine room, with wages only slightly higher than Ordinary Seamen and Messmen. The original Wiper, Charlie Taylor, became the 'Bull' Wiper.

With all that was going on I don't think I went ashore in Singapore and certainly have no memory of doing so. We weren't there very long anyway. The anchor was pulled up the next day and we steamed out of the harbor, bound for San Francisco.

A day or two after we left Singapore, I was hanging out in the messhall at noon waiting for Kay Hagen to finish up with lunch so we could play Casino. Mike Costello pushed his plate away, stood up and walked over to where I was sitting. "Anybody on here play chess," he asked.

"Yeah, I do." I was cocky about my chess ability and considered myself something of a hot-shot. My eldest sister taught me to play at a young age and I'd won a mickey mouse tournament in grammar school. I had yet to meet my match on a merchant ship.

"Want a game?" Without waiting for an answer, Mike walked over to where games were stacked next to the bulkhead. He brought back a chess board and put it down in front of me.

"Sure," I said, "if you've got five bucks to bet." At the time, $5 was a sizeable wager equivalent to a couple hours of overtime. I expected to scare off the new Wiper.

Mike pulled a sizeable wad of bills out of his pocket and slapped down a fin next to the chess board. "You're on."

I tried to fool's mate Mike but it didn't work. He was a good player. The game got pretty intense. Meanwhile, Kay Hagen played Casino with Pasquale, the 8-12 AB at a different table.

I finally beat Mike and pocketed the $5 bill about 15 minutes before he had to go back to the engine room at 1300 hours. "Good game," he said. "I'd like you to help me with a project once we get back to the States." He lowered his voice. "I'll make it worth your while."

I remember that I agreed without being told exactly what Mike's "project" was or what my "while" was worth. Like I said, Mike Costello was a very persuasive guy. I'd be a liar if I told you that I didn't think that Mike was up to something illegal, but it's true that I didn't know all the details until after he'd completed what turned out to be the latest in a series of smuggling schemes.

I don't remember a lot about the voyage back across the Pacific, except that the crew was so tense that there was a smell of mutiny. Mike Zubovich, or what was left of him, had been taken off in Singapore. Pete Ahearn was still in irons, in the spare cabin on the deck level for the Mates. I stood guard duty for overtime pay, two hours every afternoon, in another spare cabin next to the one Pete was in. I can't remember whether or not there was a way for me to communicate with Pete but I do remember that we didn't talk.

I had one less room to clean because the little Greek Third Mate was still so paranoid that he wouldn't go back to his cabin.

The Kid flipped out and stayed in his bunk. He made regular visits to the medical officer for ailments real or perceived. The Kid wouldn't talk unless he had to and could barely do his job. Sometimes he couldn't do his job at all, and I had to cover as Pantryman. I wrote down overtime for that.

The steward department did have a mutiny of sorts. Panama Frank, borderline incompetent to start with, wouldn't leave his cabin/office. Eddie Jackson called a meeting in his fo'c'sle one evening after supper. He suggested that we take a vote on replacing Panama Frank with the Chief Cook, Jimmy Coker, to become acting Steward. The vote for Mother Coker was unanimous. Even the Kid voted, though he was already of questionable mental competence. All seven of us agreed to ignore anything Panama Frank said and take orders only from Jimmy Coker. What we were agreeing to, basically, was to engage in conduct that the Coast Guard would have defined as

Insubordination, for which we could have lost our seamen's papers. With Mother Coker assigning overtime, the stores finally got organized and I got paid to clean up the little flooded storeroom. Or I thought I was getting paid. It remained to be seen whether Whistlebritches would dispute OT sheets signed by the Chief Cook.

U.S. merchant ships are required by the Coast Guard to have weekly fire and boat drills. We would take our assigned stations and run out the water hoses to prepare for fire. For sinking drills, we would assemble by our assigned lifeboats and crank out the davits to swing each lifeboat away from the deck over the water. It was during one such boat drill that the Captain's authority fell apart.

We were close to the dateline, about halfway to San Francisco, when the alarm went off one afternoon for a fire and boat drill. After the fire hoses were put away, officers and crew assembled by the lifeboats—two on each side—one deck below the bridge. My lifeboat was on the port side. In response to a steam whistle to prepare to abandon ship, two seamen manned each ratcheted crank handle for the davits—one at either end—to launch the lifeboat. In response to another steam whistle, they started cranking. Others assigned to the boat simply stood there. Wire cable on the davits lifted the lifeboat up and out of her cradle so she could swing outboard from the hull, over the ocean. It was easy to lower the lifeboat but a bitch to crank her back up. For that reason lifeboat drills were usually considered complete when the boat was swung out over the water but not lowered.

On that day, however, Whistlebritches decided to conduct the boat drill himself instead of leaving it to the Chief Mate. He came out onto the port flying bridge above us. "Lower away to the waterline," he yelled down. I don't remember who were the four deck department sailors on the crank handles but I do remember that they lowered the port lifeboat a couple of feet and then stopped. "Lower away, I said!" Whistlebritches was almost screaming. Nothing happened.

"Hey, Whistlebritches," a voice called out. Calling him that to his face was "misconduct" as defined by the Coast Guard. I recognized the voice as belonging to the Baker, Eddie Jackson. I next heard some hooting and recognized the voice of Ed Tinsley. Catcalls from others of the unlicensed crew started after that and I may have been guilty of some misconduct myself. The junior Mates and Engineers assigned to my port lifeboat stood in embarrassed silence as the jeering got louder. I don't remember Mike Costello being there. He must have been assigned to a starboard lifeboat.

Whistlebritches ran back inside the bridge, perhaps to get his . 45. Maybe he realized that the clip didn't hold enough bullets to dispatch all the insubordinates by the port lifeboat, because he didn't come out again. Instead, the Chief Mate came out onto the wing of the bridge. Mr. Marz was a mellow old salt, close to retirement. (I'll bet he wished he'd retired before getting on the Producer.) "Secure the boats," he ordered, "and go below." We obeyed that order.

Mike Costello was something of a mystery to me. I played a lot of chess with him as the Producer steamed for San Francisco. We talked but he never told me much about who he really was. He'd mostly tell me stories about working on other ships. I think he first went to sea in 1966. Mike had some good tales about dealing with SIU goons—bully-boys who were usually Italian—in the late '60s back at union headquarters in New York. On a personal level, the most I got out of him was that he was a military brat, as am I. But one time when we were talking, Mike told me his recipe for happiness: "Something to do, something to hope for, and someone to love."

It was only later that I realized that Mike was a professional smuggler.

V

The S.S. Producer passed underneath the Golden Gate Bridge and I could finally smell land again.

Two Customs agents performed a cursory search of the Producer after we lowered the gangway in San Francisco and then told the officers and crew to line up in the messhall after breakfast to declare our souvenirs. Several F.B.I. agents swarmed aboard at 0645 before Customs cleared the ship. Kay Hagen was jonesing for a drink and offered me a sizeable bribe if I'd go ashore to buy him a jug of blended whiskey. I slipped down the gangway and went looking for a liquor store. While I was gone, Pete Ahearn was taken off the ship in handcuffs and F.B.I. agents interviewed my shipmates. I'm glad to have missed that, even though I didn't know nearly as much then as I know now. Ed Tinsley told me later that the agents were digging desperately for a motive for the murder, questioning relentlessly about homosexuality and drugs. They didn't seem to understand the concept of "too much seatime" and tight quarters for long periods cause strange behavior. Mike Costello cooled his heels and wouldn't make his move until later. I don't know whether he was interviewed by the F.B.I. or not.

Also while I was ashore, the Kid was taken off the ship in a strait-jacket. I heard he was taken to a mental hospital. I've never seen the Kid since and don't know what happened to him.

When I came back to the ship, carrying a half-gallon of Canadian Mist, I saw two ABs hanging over the stern on separate stages—dangling planks—repainting the name of our ship. I lingered until I made out "American Rice" being painted on the hull. The S.S. Producer was no more.

Certificate of Discharge to Merchant Seaman

DEPARTMENT OF TRANSPORTATION
UNITED STATES COAST GUARD

Serial No. I 7205634

I HEREBY CERTIFY that the above entries were made by me and are correct and that the signatures hereto were witnessed by me.

Dated this 31st day of March, 1972.

United States Shipping Commissioner.
(or Master of Vessel)

Note—Whenever a master performs the duties of the shipping commissioner under this act, the master shall sign the certification on the line designated for the shipping commissioner's signature.
534-56-2121

Name of Seaman John W. Merriam
Citizenship U.S.A. U. S. Merchant Mariners Document No. Z 534562121
Rating Utility/Messman (Capacity in which employed)
Date of Shipment 22 December 1971
Place of Shipment Portland, Oregon
Date of Discharge 31 March 1972
Place of Discharge San Francisco, California
Name of Ship PRODUCER
Name of Employer American Rice Steamship Co.
Official No. 245888 Class of Vessel Steam (Steam, Motor, Sail or Barge)
Nature of Voyage Foreign (Foreign, Intercoastal or Coastwise)

We signed off foreign articles in San Francisco on March 31, 1972. Most of the crew, including Mike Costello, quit as soon as they were paid off. It turned out that the load of rice in Sacramento fell through or was an unfounded rumor to begin with. The S.S. American Rice was to return to Washington State to pick up more grain for delivery to god-knows-where. I signed coastwise articles, as did most in the steward department, so I could get closer to home. When under coastwise articles, a seaman can quit at any port in the U.S.

We steamed up the coast, crested the Columbia Bar, and tied up next to grain silos in Kalama, on the Washington side of the Columbia River. As soon as the gangway was lowered, there was

Mike Costello coming back aboard. With him was a tall man with a black mustache.

Mike called me on my promise and told me to follow him. I went down to the engine room with him and the tall man to the paint locker. The paint locker was an enclosure about 10-foot-square, walled off by thick wire in a large mesh pattern.

"Look out for Charlie Taylor and the new Oiler, or the Third Assistant," Mike told me as he and the tall man went into the paint locker. Acting as lookout, I watched through the mesh as they pried off the tops to five-gallon paint buckets until they found the one they were looking for. Mike fished out a large lump from a bucket of white paint. He removed the contents from a paint-soaked plastic bag and dropped the plastic back into the bucket. "Let's go."

I wouldn't know for some time exactly what Mike pulled out of that bucket of paint but I'd promised to help. I followed him and the tall man up to the main deck, down the gangway, and to a car out on the wharf. Thanks for your help, John," Mike said as the tall man got into the car and took the wheel. Mike pulled a wad out of his pocket and peeled off 15 C-notes. "I'll be in touch," he said as he handed them to me. Then he and the tall man sped off in the car. That $1,500 was the most money I'd ever held in my hand at one time.

I stayed on the S.S. American Rice until we got a little closer to Seattle at our next port—Longview, Washington, downriver on the Columbia—and quit just before the crew signed foreign articles for another voyage. It was April 6, 1972.

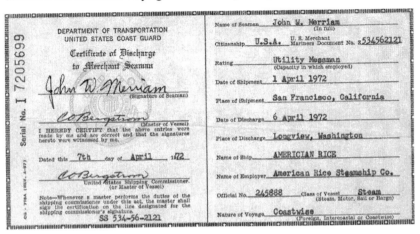

I got cheated out of overtime wages for organizing stores and cleaning up the flooded storeroom. Whistlebritches disputed it, saying my OT sheets were illegal because they were signed by the Chief Cook instead of the Steward. 'I still did the work,' I thought bitterly. 'Why should the Aliotos get free labor because of a technicality?' Before walking down the gangway for the last time, I grabbed a top-of-the-line French knife, meat cleaver and wood-handled sharpening steel, and stuck them in my seabag. I figured that made us even.

Eddie Jackson had somehow gotten his Cadillac from Seattle to the dock in Longview. Ed Tinsley, Kay Hagen and I piled in and rode the 125 miles back to Seattle in style.

Once in Seattle, I went to Poke's Cycle and paid $1580 cash for a brand-new Norton 750 Commando Roadster.

VI

I tried to forget about what happened on the S.S. Producer. Four months later I was living in a rental house in the Magnolia District of Seattle, shacked up with a woman from California, when a strange man came to my door and served me with a subpoena.

I was summoned to the trial of United States v. Peter Ahearn. The subpoena "commanded" that I testify in San Francisco at the United States District Court on Golden Gate Avenue on September 11, 1972.

United States District Court

FOR THE
NORTHERN DISTRICT OF CALIFORNIA

UNITED STATES OF AMERICA

v.

PETER RAYMOND AHEARN

FORMA PAUPERIS

No. 72-398 SW

To
John W. Merriam
4611-34th Street West
Seattle, Washington 98199

You are hereby commanded to appear in the United States District Court for the Northern Courtroom of Spencer Williams
District of California at 450 Golden Gate Avenue in the city of

San Francisco on the 11th day of September 19 72 at 10:00 o'clock A M. to

testify in the above-entitled case.

This subpoena is issued on application of the[1] defendant

August 7, 19 72.

Frank O. Bell, Jr., Chief AFPD
Attorney for Defendant
450 Golden Gate Avenue
Address San Francisco, CA. 94102
Telephone: (415) 556-7712

Clerk.

By
Deputy Clerk.

RETURN

Received this subpoena at on
and on at I served it on the
within named
by delivering a copy to and tendering[2] to the fee for one day's attendance and the mileage
allowed by law.

By

Service Fees

Travel _____ $
Services _____ $
Total _____ $

[1] Insert "United States," or "defendant" as the case may be.
[2] Fees and mileage need not be tendered to the witness upon service of a subpoena issued in behalf of the United States or an officer or agency thereof. 28 USC 1825, or on behalf of a defendant who is financially unable to pay such costs (Rule 17(b), Federal Rules Criminal Procedure).

The subpoena was signed by the lawyer for the defendant, Frank Bell "AFPD"—whatever that meant. I figured Pete must be the defendant, but I didn't know why his lawyer wanted me to testify. I called the phone number on the subpoena, collect.

After some rigmarole and returned calls I ended up talking to a guy who said he was an investigator for the public defender's office in San Francisco. He asked me general questions about the Producer's crew, like who was friends with whom, and got cagey when asked why the public defender wanted my testimony. The investigator said I'd be paid for food and lodging, plus 16 cents per mile for traveling to and from San Francisco for the trial.

I decided to combine subpoena compliance with a motorcycle trip and rode to San Francisco on my new Norton.

The trial got postponed and I arrived there on September 20th. After asking directions, I found the federal courthouse, which was in the middle of downtown San Francisco. I wasn't allowed into the courtroom until it was my turn to testify and waited on one of the benches in the hallway outside. I don't remember who of my shipmates were there, but one of them—it might have been the Day Man, Pat Ryan—told me the Pantryman ('the Kid') had just left the courtroom after testifying. He also told me that, according to the Captain's testimony, Ahearn killed Zubovich with a marlin spike. The Old Man told the jury that he based his opinion on the appearance of the wounds and his claim that a 20-inch marlin spike was missing from the Bo's'n locker. Pete, on the other hand, testified after the Captain that he'd killed Zubovich with a home-made spear.

According to my shipmate, Pete didn't deny killing Mike Zubovich, and even admitted planning it. He told the jury that he knew of the Ordinary Seaman's reputation and was afraid of him. Pete described the confrontation and the words exchanged over the Ordinary's missed gangway watches in Bandar Abbas. When Mike Zubovich told Pete he was going to kill him, Pete decided the only way to protect himself was to kill the Ordinary first. Pete then gave the jury elaborate detail about fashioning a spear in the engine room and hiding it until the time was right. He explained the watch system to the jury and how long it was before his last look-out on the 4-8 watch coincided with the Ordinary's first look-out on the 8-12. The prosecutor made Pete give the jury the gory description of the murder itself and got him to admit that he'd planned to toss the Ordinary's body over the side, into the ocean, so his killing of Mike Zubovich would never be revealed. The prosecutor also got Pete to admit that he was surprised at how the Ordinary was able to outrun him on the main deck when he was gushing blood from several puncture wounds.

I can't remember the reaction to Pete's testimony from the shipmate who told me this, but I remember mine: Pete was trying to bullshit the jury into finding that he killed Mike Zubovich in self-defense. I wasn't afraid of the Ordinary and there was no reason that an ex-Marine like Pete Ahearn should have been. Never mentioned was the strange effect upon men's minds from long periods at sea in close proximity to each other. 'It's simple,' I thought. 'Too much seatime. The motive is that Zubovich got on Pete's nerves, so Pete killed him. The jury won't have too much trouble convicting him.' I wondered why the public defender wanted me to testify.

The courtroom itself, once I was allowed in, was large with high ceilings and ornate fixtures on the walls. I was on the witness stand for all of ten minutes. The public defender asked some background questions about me and being on the Producer and then cut to the chase: "Did you ever hear Mike Zubovich say he was going to kill somebody?"

"Sure, he said that to me and a lot of other people," I answered. "But that's—"

"No further questions." The public defender cut me off. I was trying to say that that's the way Mike spoke to everybody and no one took it seriously. I figured the prosecutor would ask me to explain, even though the prosecutor hadn't tried to talk to me before.

The prosecutor asked me no questions and I was excused from the witness stand.

After testifying, I was allowed to stay in the courtroom and watch the rest of the trial. The public defender put on a string of witnesses he'd brought up from Houston. They told the jury in gruesome detail about how Mike Zubovich had pulled a guy off a barstool and beat his brains out, literally, with a baseball bat in 1970. It was powerful testimony and I watched the jurors recoil in horror.

The jury was out less than eight hours and came back with a verdict of Not Guilty. I guess the jurors thought Zubovich was such a low-life that Pete had performed a service to society by killing him.

I was upset by the verdict. The killing of Mike Zubovich by Pete Ahearn was premeditated murder. The only explanation for the jury's verdict that I could think of was that the prosecutor got out-lawyered by the public defender.

I turned 21 years old riding my motorcycle back to Seattle from the trial.

I stayed in the merchant marine for another 10 years.

I think Mike Zubovich had more brothers, in addition to Steve Troy, the union patrolman. I heard scuttlebutt in the union hall that the Zubovich brothers settled the score with Pete Ahearn. I don't know if that's true or not, but I never saw Pete again.

Kay Hagen drank himself to death a few years later. I last saw Chester in the late '70s or early '80s, in the hiring hall. Semi-coherently, he rambled about having just been let out of Harborview Hospital after downing a half-gallon of whiskey. I never sailed again with any of my shipmates from the Producer, although I saw some of them around the union hall. No one wanted to talk much about that ship.

I saw Mike Costello now and then but he never asked me to help with another smuggling operation. Had he asked, I can't honestly tell you what I would have said.

VII

I quit the merchant marine in 1982, got married, bought a house, and took a job on land. Mike Costello didn't settle down and kept living in the fast lane. He was always a mystery figure and showed up unexpectedly at odd times over the years to invite me for a drink or a game of chess. He told me fantastic stories but never spoke directly about drug deals, and I could only guess where he was getting his money.

Mike went back to sea, off and on, usually sailing as Electrician. I had assumed he only caught ships as part of smuggling ventures but by the 1990s I got the impression that his luck was slipping and wages were his only source of income.

Into the 2000s—however one is supposed to label that decade —Mike's luck was slipping more. The law had always been nipping at his heels, but by then various police-types were closing in and Mike sometimes acted like he had a hellhound on his trail. He was hyperactive and talked too fast. He'd always been gregarious and very generous, especially in bars, but now I started picking up the tab.

Mike married twice to beautiful women—I met them both— and fathered a son by each. I'm not sure if it was drugs and alcohol, or some itch that Mike could never scratch, but he lost all of them—his wives and his boys. I think he forgot his own definition of happiness. Mike certainly had 'something to do' and he probably had 'something to hope for'—although I'm not sure what that was toward the end, other than staying out of prison. It was 'someone to love' that Mike was missing. He threw away two families.

The last time I saw Mike was earlier that year—2006, I think it was in the spring—when he came into my office at Seattle's Fishermen's Terminal. Mike still walked jauntily but it seemed a little forced. "Hey, John, I just got released from a federal prison in Eastern Oregon. Loan me ten bucks so I can pay my tab at Chinook's." Chinook's is a restaurant and bar at Fishermen's Terminal.

"OK." I handed him a $20 bill. "How'd you get them to serve you with no money?"

"After I downed a couple drinks, I told the bartender that I was good friends with a mucky-muck in the West Wall Building." Mike winked at me. "I gave him my driver's license and told him I'd be back with the money in 10 minutes.

"That prison was something," he went on. "There were gangs of white guys, blacks, and Chicanos. You didn't get to choose sides. You were automatically enrolled as soon as you walked through the gate."

"How'd you end up there?" I asked.

"A peckerhead of an Ass't U.S. Attorney has been on my ass, claiming that I lied on a Coast Guard form that I'm not a drug addict and that, therefore, I'm guilty of a felony . . . " Mike continued describing the legal case against him, which he said was phony. I couldn't quite keep up with all the details. But then, I'd never been able to completely follow Mike's descriptions about his involvement with the legal system.

Mike left my office to pay his bar tab. I never saw him again.

EPILOGUE

Mike Costello's luck ran out for good on August 17, 2006. He was shot to death in a car underneath the West Seattle Bridge. It's still listed officially as an unsolved homicide, but I can guess what Mike was doing when he got shot—making a drug deal. Where he got killed was west of Harbor Island at the entrance to Pier 5, the old Sea-Land dock where Mike—and me, too—walked onto many a containership.

Mike Costello's ashes were sprinkled into Puget Sound from a ferry on the Vashon Island run. Farewell, Mike.

24843284R00046

Made in the USA
Middletown, DE
08 October 2015